DISCARD

AN ALBUM OF
MODERN CHINA

AN ALBUM OF
MODERN CHINA

BY FREDERICK KING POOLE

FRANKLIN WATTS
New York | London | Toronto | Sydney
1981

A GROLIER COMPANY

Frontis: the Great Wall of China snakes through the mountains north and west of Peking.

Maps by Vantage Art

Cover photographs courtesy of Xinhua News Agency.

Photographs courtesy of United Press International: opp. page 1, 9 (top right), 16 (top), 21 (bottom), 43, 51 (bottom), 67 (bottom), 76, 83 (top); Wide World Photos: pp. 10 (bottom right), 23; Library of Congress: p. 40; U.S. Army: p. 44; The New York Public Library Picture Collection: pp. 6 (bottom right), 18, 22 (top), 24 (top), 28 (all), 31 (both), 32 (both), 35, 36, 37, 39 (both), 58 (top), 67 (center), 86 (top); Xinhua News Agency: frontis, 5 (top and bottom), 6 (top and bottom left), 9 (top left and bottom), 10 (top and bottom left), 11 (both), 13 (both), 14 (both), 16 (bottom), 17 (both), 21 (top), 22 (bottom), 24 (bottom), 27, 46, 47 (both), 48 (both), 51 (top), 52 (both), 54, 57 (both), 58 (bottom), 59 (both), 61, 63 (all), 64 (all), 65 (both), 67 (top), 68 (all), 69 (all), 71 (both), 72, 75 (both), 77, 79, 80, 82 (both), 83 (bottom), 85 (both), 86 (bottom), 87.

Library of Congress
Cataloging in Publication Data

Poole, Frederick King.
An album of modern China.

Includes index.
SUMMARY: Discusses life in China before and after the Communist revolution, stressing the importance of the country's cultural heritage.
1. China—Juvenile literature. [1. China]
I. Title.
DS706.P66   951   80–25081
ISBN 0–531–01502–5

CONTENTS

(1)
THE MIDDLE KINGDOM

With thousands of years of recorded history behind them, the people of China participate in what is today the world's oldest continuing civilization. With close to a billion inhabitants, China has by far the largest population of any of the world's nations. With a land area of nearly 3.7 million square miles (9.5 million sq km), stretching about 2,000 miles (3,200 km) north to south and more than 3,000 miles (3,800 km) east to west, it covers more of the earth's surface than any other country except the Soviet Union or Canada.

China is a land self-contained and culturally distinct from all other nations. Traditionally the Chinese have considered their nation to be the center of the world. For this reason they have called it the Middle Kingdom, or *Chung-Kuo,* and the Celestial Empire. Although innumerable dialects are spoken, the written language, which historically consists of a total of some 40,000 characters (in recent years simplified and reduced to 10,000 characters, with the average Chinese knowing about 3,000 to 5,000), representing words and ideas, is the same all over China.

Today the People's Republic of China is united under a Communist government, which has as its capital the majestic ancient city in the north, Peking. In the past China has more often than not been similarly united under the emperors of various dynasties, that is, ruling families and conquering political factions. Some strong dynasties stayed in power for many centuries.

THE DIVERSITY OF CHINA

Despite the unity of the Chinese nation, however, there have always been, and there still are, distinctions between the inner China and the outer China. The inner China is the homeland of the Han people, a predominantly agricultural race that makes up 94 percent of the Chinese population. The outer China, containing mostly mi-

**Mount Lushan
in China's Kiangsi Province
overlooks the Yangtze River
on the north.**

CHINA AND SOUTHEAST ASIA

U.S.S.R.

Harbin •

SEA
OF
JAPAN

MANCHURIA

NORTH
KOREA

MONGOLIA

Mukden •

JAPAN

Peking •   • Dairen

SOUTH
KOREA

N. China Plains

GOBI
DESERT

Tientsin

Yellow

YELLOW
SEA

SINKIANG

River

AFGHANISTAN

Yenan •

CHINA

Yellow River Valley

Nanking •   • Shanghai

Hankow

PAKISTAN

Hanyang •   • Wuchang

Hangchow

EAST
CHINA
SEA

Yangtze River

• Chungking

TIBET

Amoy •

TAIWAN

MOUNT
EVEREST

Swaton •

NEPAL •   BHUTAN

Pearl River

Canton

YUNNAN

Hong Kong

INDIA

PAKISTAN

NORTH
VIETNAM

HAINAN
ISLAND

MANILA

BURMA

LAOS

SOUTH
CHINA
SEA

THAILAND

CAMBODIA

SOUTH
VIETNAM

CEYLON

MALAYSIA

PACIFIC
OCEAN

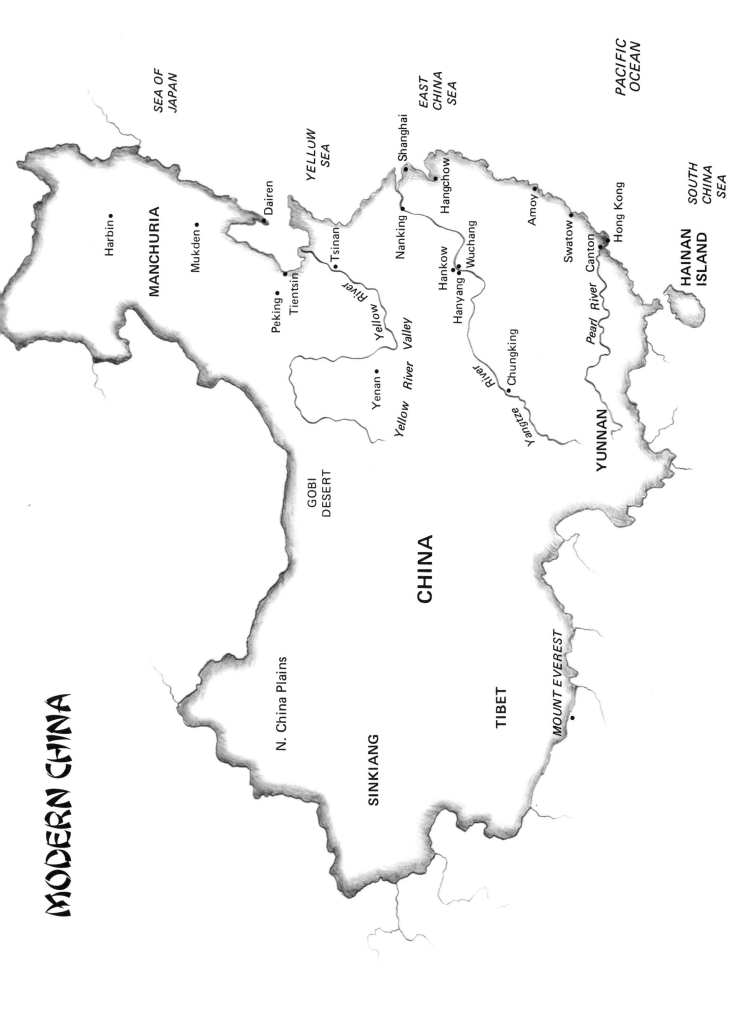

MODERN CHINA

SEA OF JAPAN

YELLOW SEA

EAST CHINA SEA

PACIFIC OCEAN

SOUTH CHINA SEA

MANCHURIA

Harbin

Mukden

Dairen

Peking

Tientsin

Tsinan

Nanking

Shanghai

Hangchow

Amoy

Swatow

Canton

Hong Kong

HAINAN ISLAND

Hankow
Wuchang
Hanyang

Chungking

Yenan

Yellow River Valley

Yellow River

Yangtze River

Pearl River

GOBI DESERT

N. China Plains

SINKIANG

CHINA

TIBET

YUNNAN

MOUNT EVEREST

nority peoples, is made up of vast regions in the far north and west. Many of these minority groups were, by tradition, warriors and nomads who wandered from place to place in search of grazing land for their livestock.

There are also distinct, though lesser, cultural differences between the Han who live in the northern part of inner China and the Han who live in the south.

Inner China, or the heartland of China, is the territory that we usually think of when the subject of China arises. To get an idea of what it includes, start on a map with the city of Harbin in Manchuria in the northeast. Draw an imaginary line southwest through the capital, Peking, down to the city of Chungking. Then draw an imaginary line southeast to the coast and around to Hainan Island. Connect Hainan to Chungking. This curved triangle, including the coasts on the East China and South China seas and an entrance to the Pacific Ocean, is roughly the land of the Han people.

But there is another China west and north of the triangle. Although sparsely populated, it is larger in land area than the heartland and consists mainly of dry mountains and deserts. The people of the far north and west are more likely to be engaged in raising livestock than in the planting and plowing that go on in inner China.

The heartland, where the Han people live, is made up of river valleys, rolling plains, spectacular mountains, and deep gorges. The northern and southern parts of the heartland are separated by the more than 3,400-mile (5,470-km)-long Yangtze River. The Yangtze runs through deep gorges in the west, then flows eastward into the lush ricelands of central China, where it supplies the water for many lakes. It finally empties into the East China Sea at the great port city of Shanghai.

At Nanking there is a high bridge—the pride of the nation—built over the Yangtze in the 1960s. Originally the bridge was to be built with assistance from the USSR, but disputes led to the cutting off of Soviet aid, and the Chinese went ahead alone. This bridge is so high that 10,000-ton (9,000-m.t.) ships can pass beneath it. But generally communications between the north and south are still inadequate.

The land of the Han people is so intensely farmed that virtually no areas where food can be grown go to waste. About a quarter of China is suited to farming. Although exact figures are hard to get, probably about 300 million acres (121 million hectares) are now under cultivation. Besides farmland, China is rich in coal and iron ore

(4)

Top: coal from the Fuhsin Mines in Liaoning Province is loaded on railway cars for delivery. Bottom left: a new concrete dam harnesses the power of the Yellow River at Chingtung Gorge. Bottom right: in the late 1970s, the Chinese farmer still used a water buffalo and plow to till his lands.

and has started exporting oil. It has abundant reserves of the minerals manganese and tungsten and large amounts of tin and asbestos, though copper, zinc, lead, and nickel are in short supply. Tea, the national drink, is of course cultivated throughout the nation.

Irrigation is needed for about half of the farmland. Sometimes the water for irrigation is pumped through canals and spillways. Often it is carried in buckets. This is one of the reasons why Chinese peasant farmers have such a long tradition of cooperating with each other. It is also why they have tended to accept the necessity for a higher authority, because disputes concerning the distribution of water and the maintenance of dikes must be settled.

China's civilization began along the Yellow River Valley in the north. It spread first along the North China plains, where the farmland is extremely rich, and then east. The seasons are well defined in this part of China. The winter begins in late November, with freezing winds coming from Manchuria and the Gobi Desert in the north. The first signs of spring come in mid-February. The summers can be unpleasantly hot.

In the south, where civilization spread more gradually, the winters are milder, and the summers are hotter and more humid. The far south is almost tropical and has a great deal of rain.

The northern part of the Chinese heartland is where the dialect that serves as the nation's official spoken language (taught in the schools throughout China) is most commonly used. This dialect is generally known as Mandarin. Many other dialects are also spoken in the north, and in the south spoken dialects can change practically from village to village.

Because only one written language is used by all of China, in cities it is common to see Chinese who cannot understand each other's spoken dialects communicating by written notes.

THE RURAL LIFE

In the north, before Communism, some of the farms were relatively large. A farmer using a donkey or a mule could plant up to twelve acres of wheat or the cereal grass millet. In the south, the most common work animal is the long-horned water buffalo, which is also the most common work animal in the surrounding countries of Southeast Asia. Rice, again as in much of Southeast Asia, is the staple of the southern diet. It is planted by hand. Rice shoots are then transplanted to fields that are completely submerged in water. The mud dikes that hold in the water are also built and tended by hand. The most land an individual southern Chinese rice farmer, with the help of his or her family, could cultivate this way, plowing with water buffalo and doing the rest of the work by hand, was about three acres.

In the north, there are domestic sheep and goats on the mountainsides and cattle on the flat lands. In the south, livestock, in addition to the water buffalo, consists mainly of pigs, chickens, and ducks.

Out beyond the heartland are the vast and wild regions of Tibet in the west, Sinkiang in the northwest, and Inner Mongolia in the north. These are officially called Autonomous Regions, meaning that in theory they are allowed a certain amount of self-government. At various times during past eras they have, in effect, been separate nations, and their warriors frequently attacked and sometimes conquered the heartland. But over the centuries China's rulers have considered them to be an integral part of China. Emperors were not believed to have ruled all of China until they conquered the outer regions. Today these regions are firmly under the control of Peking. Elsewhere in China, now also under central government control, are many non-Han, essentially tribal, people. Some, such as the Hakkas in the south, who are skilled fishermen, have a history of piracy.

In China as a whole, there are about two hundred people per square mile. This is about half the population density of New York State. Of course the heartland of China is far more densely populated than that. But in the desert and wild mountain regions of Tibet, Sinkiang, and Inner Mongolia, the population density is generally only about ten persons per square mile, and in vast stretches of these outer regions the population is even less dense than that. In one of China's geographically wildest areas sits Mount Everest, at 29,028 feet (8,847 m) the world's highest mountain. Mount Everest is shared by China's Tibet and the small nation of Nepal, located between China and India.

Many farms in the north are large, but because of overcrowded conditions a typical northern peasant family in pre-Communist China was forced to earn a living from only three acres, often as little as one acre, of land. In the United States, in contrast, a family farm varies in size from 200 to 450 acres (80 to 182 hectares). (A more typical farm in the United States, however, is owned by a corporation and is much larger.) Today in China, the average peasant farmer is part of a commune, a larger community that combines a great many of what were once individual farms.

(8)

Top left: vast terraces make optimum use of land
for growing rice on a commune in Kweichow
Province. Top right: workers in the Yunnan Province
painstakingly weed the rice fields. Bottom: members
of a commune in Inner Mongolia tend their livestock.

Top: a herdsman looks on as sheep and horses graze in present-day Inner Mongolia, a scene that could also have taken place many years ago. Bottom left: fur-hatted horsemen survey the land from a snowy hill in a remote part of Inner Mongolia. Bottom right: a view of Tibet as seen from the highest spot on earth, the top of 29,082-foot (8,864 m) Mt. Everest.

**Top: bicyclists halt at an
intersection during rush hour
in Peking. Bottom: ships travel
along the Hwang Pu River to
China's largest city, Shanghai.**

Most Chinese farmers today, in addition, make their homes in towns and villages. They set out on foot or by bicycle each morning to work their fields. Many larger cities have as their principal economic activity commerce in rural products.

THE GREAT CITIES

In spite of its strong agricultural bent, however, China still has its great cities. The port city of Shanghai at the estuary of the Yangtze River on the East China Sea has a population of more than ten million. Before the Communist takeover in the late 1940s, Shanghai was one of the world's most important centers for international shipping and trading. Today, under the Communist government, there is much less international commerce in Shanghai. China's major center for foreign shipping is actually the British colony of Hong Kong at the nation's southern tip, which has a population perhaps as high as six million. But Shanghai, according to United Nations calculations, is the largest city in the world.

To the northeast of Shanghai is Peking, which is probably the world's most stately capital city. Its some eight million people live in or near great open squares, broad avenues, and vast, paved courtyards. Peking is still dominated by a cluster of golden-roofed and tiled palaces known collectively as the Forbidden City and serving as the traditional seat of the central government.

The major port in the south is Canton, with about five million inhabitants, the site of trade fairs where people from all over the world congregate to do business with the Chinese. Canton is located on the Pearl River and is a short trip by boat from the sleepy Portuguese coastal enclave of Macao or by train from Hong Kong. Canton has none of the impressive architecture of Peking, but it is an important international commercial center and has been the place in China most frequently visited by foreign business people.

Between Canton and Shanghai are the old coastal cities of Swatow, Foochow, and Amoy, which still have cobblestone streets. In these cities the mountains come right down to the harbors. More of South China than North China is broken up by mountains. The resulting isolation of people in South China explains why there are so many distinct southern dialects that cannot be understood except in the immediate areas where they are used.

Top: the facade of the Chairman Mao Memorial
Hall is an impressive addition to the large
T'ien An Men Square in Peking. Bottom: rapeseed
plants, from which a type of oil is made, are
in full bloom across from a modern port and
industrial area in a Shanghai suburb.

Top: the light flow of Peking's motorized traffic
has more than ample room on this city's streets.
Bottom: the imposing mausoleum of Dr. Sun
Yat-sen is a tribute to the revolutionary who led
the overthrow of the old Imperial regime several
decades before the Communists came to power.

Another important city is Hangchow, in Chekiang Province. Just south of Shanghai, Hangchow is built around many restful lakes. Just east of Shanghai, in Kiangsu Province, is Nanking, the former capital of Nationalist China, the first real government to follow the last imperial dynasty. The Nationalists clung to power until the Communists took over in the years after World War II. Nanking has many modern public buildings. It is dominated by a hill containing the mausoleum of the founder of the Nationalist government, Sun Yatsen. During wartime the Nationalist capital was moved west to the muggy city of Chungking in China's remote but heavily populated province of Szechuan.

Near Peking, the city of Tientsin, formerly a center for British and Japanese trading activity, still has many European town houses, a British-style park beside a town hall, and a clock tower made from imported stone.

These cities have traditionally been administrative or trading centers. Because outside penetration of the country was so great in the century before the Communists came to power, they all show, to varying degrees, remnants of foreign cultures. In Manchuria in the northeast, the original homeland of the last imperial rulers, the cities are distinguished by Japanese colonial architecture. And there is still, in what is now Heilungkiang Province, a certain international flavor to the Manchurian city of Harbin, a quarter of which was once populated by refugees from the Russian Revolution.

The monotonous factory cities of Hankow, Wuchang, and Hanyang, in Hupei Province, make up what is known as the Wuhan complex—the principal industrial complex and largest metropolis of central China. However, in spite of its scenic location at the junction of the Han and Yangtze rivers, in general the Wuhan complex and China's other important industrial cities—such as Tsinan in Shantung Province in the east, and also Tientsin and the formerly cosmopolitan Manchurian cities of Mukden, Harbin, and Dairen—give the impression of what one observer has called "a sooty, gray sprawl." They are built around industrial plants and railroad yards.

It must always be remembered, however, that after the Communist revolution big cities in China were considered less important than the countryside. The late Mao Tse-tung, leader of the revolution and Chairman of the Chinese Communist party until his death in 1976, advocated a policy he called *hsai fang*, which involved moving people from the city to the country. Chairman Mao (family names come first in Chinese) always spoke of the revolution as favoring the

Left: despite the rather ancient-looking equipment at this shop on a Canton street, the barber appears to be happily getting his job done. Below: in a commune in Kiangsu Province, women harvest silk cocoons. Silkworm cultivation is a traditional sideline occupation.

Top: lights are reflected in the waters
of the Yangtze River at Chungking,
formerly the Nationalists' wartime
capital. Bottom: fresh fruits and
vegetables are plentiful in the middle
of winter at Tientsin's main market.

country's peasant farmers. The virtues of peasant life are continually praised in modern China.

Still, city life has been for centuries, and remains, an important part of the life of China as a whole. And it is sure to become an increasingly important factor if the nation's leaders continue as they are doing to push for ever greater industrialization.

It is interesting that so much remains in the cities that reflects China's past. One feature of the old cities was that their central portions were surrounded by high walls. The streets were orderly, following the pattern of the walls. Remnants of these walls still stand. The old practice of setting aside an entire street for a particular trade—such as Silk Street or Jade Street—is still followed. In many of the smaller cities and towns the streets are still unpaved. Most are lined by the walls that surrounded government offices, business establishments, schools, and private residences.

THE INTERNATIONAL FRONTIERS

For that matter, much of the 1,500-mile (2,454-km)-long Great Wall of China, the largest man-made structure on earth, still stands. Built as a series of walls during the Ch'in Dynasty (221–206 B.C.), a short dynasty marked by conquest that established the borders of the Chinese empire, the Great Wall was designed to protect what were then China's northern frontiers. In its present form it dates mainly from the Ming Dynasty (A.D. 1368–1644). The Communists reconstructed the section north of Peking. The Great Wall is so large that a roadway running down its center was often used to rush troops to areas threatened by foreign invasion.

China's borders now take in much of the area beyond the wall where outside marauders used to stage their attacks. The nation at this time has 12,427 miles (19,883 km) of international boundaries. As in ancient times, it still jealously guards its northern frontiers, which it now shares with the USSR, the Soviet-backed state of Outer

Entire industrial areas of China often lie under a layer of soot and dust.

Mongolia, and North Korea. In recent years there have been border clashes with the USSR.

In the west there is a very short border with Afghanistan, and in the west and south a long one with India and the small states of Nepal, Sikkim (now part of India), and Bhutan. In 1962 China fought a border war with India.

In the far south there are borders with Burma, Laos, and Vietnam. The borders with Laos and Vietnam, both Soviet-supported states, have been very tense. In 1979 Chinese troops actually invaded the northern part of Vietnam.

Also, the point just south of China's Yunnan Province where Burma, Thailand, and Laos come together has been an especially tense area. This region is called the Golden Triangle because it is the source of much of the world's opium, the narcotic contained in poppy plants and from which the deadly drug heroin is made. Much of this section is under the control of bandits who were in the Chinese Nationalist army during the fighting between the Nationalists and the Communists in the first half of the twentieth century.

On the east, China faces the island of Taiwan, where the Nationalist government fled when it lost control of mainland China. The mainland Chinese say that Taiwan is a traditional part of China and should be reunited with it under Communist rule. The government on Taiwan claims itself to be the legitimate government of all China.

But although the army is active everywhere in China, with troops even working in the fields as farmhands, military confrontations are far removed from the day-to-day life of the ordinary Chinese peasant, who lives in what is perhaps physically the most spectacular country on earth. The mountains and river gorges in the heartland of China have had such a strong influence on Chinese artists that great landscape painting is a significant part of China's rich cultural heritage.

Above: the Great Wall of China is the largest man-made structure on earth. Below: Chairman Mao wore a coolie hat while standing in a grain field during his inspection tour of the countryside in Honan Province.

Facing page top: Chinese farmers carry their wares in baskets
hanging from poles balanced on their shoulders. Bottom: a view
of Kaohsiung Harbor, a major port on the island of Taiwan. Above:
the past and present often exist side by side in Chinese life. Hand-
drawn carts are parked in front of modern living quarters in Peking.

To the average Chinese, despite vast political, economic, and social upheavals, many aspects of daily life have remained the same for centuries. Hand-pulled carts and baskets hanging from poles carried on the shoulders are still more common than delivery vans in the cities. Donkeys, mules, and water buffalo far outnumber tractors on the farms.

Yet at the same time, China in the second half of the twentieth century has undergone drastic and dramatic changes that few observers living during the first half of the century could have dreamed of.

Above: this Chinese woman carries her children in baskets balanced on her shoulders. Below: China enters the age of television! Shoppers inspect Chinese-made television sets at an appliance store in Shanghai.

(2)
THE CHINESE HERITAGE

Historians and political commentators are continually making comparisons between the China of the past and the China of the present. The Communists who now rule China talk constantly of how they are breaking with tradition. There seem at first to be two very different sides to modern China. Yet it is possible to look upon China in such a way that both sides make sense.

Scholars outside China have always made much of the fact that, after the Communist forces took over, their leader, the late Mao Tse-tung, became a cult figure, meaning that he was practically worshipped by his people. He came to symbolize the revolution and everything the Communists were trying to accomplish. High officials as well as school children memorized and repeated over and over the writings of Mao. Many scholars point out, however, that in China's past, strong new rulers were *always* thought to be right. Hence, according to this view, Mao was following in the footsteps of the ancient emperors.

In the past, a successful emperor was said to have the Mandate of Heaven. Although the Communists oppose religious beliefs, Mao's personal leadership was so built up that, for all practical purposes, his people came to believe that he, too, had the Mandate of Heaven.

It would be unwise to conclude that everything about modern China can be understood in terms of ancient China. But at the same time it is often impossible to understand why the Chinese Communist government acts the way it does without some understanding of China's unusual history.

One reason that so many recent visitors to China from other parts of the world have found the Chinese so confident, even boastful, in their attitude is that the Chinese themselves are very much aware of their history. They attained great heights of civilization during periods when the Western world was, by any reckoning, predominantly backward, undeveloped, and barbaric.

To the Chinese people, the late Mao Tse-tung became a symbol of the revolution.

Left: a bronze relic from the Shang Dynasty (1766 to 1122 B.C.). Above left: this bronze mask was discovered in eastern China in the tomb of a ruler of the Shang Dynasty. Above right: a bronze dragon from the late Chou Dynasty. Right: this bronze ceremonial vessel from the Shang Dynasty illustrates the beautiful and detailed work done by the Chinese people during this period. Below right: a bronze water buffalo from the Chou Dynasty.

THE SPREAD OF CIVILIZATION

The origins of Chinese civilization along the Yellow River Valley have been traced back 6,000 years. At a still-early stage in their history, perhaps 3,000 years ago, the Chinese gave up the idea of an aristocracy based on birth. They then developed standards for government that seem advanced even today.

They decided that those who governed should do so on merit. Eventually top officials were required to pass competitive examinations. A system of centralized rule by highly educated men had become firmly established in China before the Christian era. Rule based on merit means rule by the people who are most qualified, rather than by the military or by people born into royal families. This was rare anywhere in the West until the late eighteenth century, and clearly it is not universal yet.

The history of China as we know it from actual records begins more than 3,500 years ago. It starts with the Shang Dynasty, which lasted from 1766 to 1122 B.C. It is from relics of the Shang period that archaeologists have found the beginnings of the Chinese written language. These early writings show that the country at that time was dominated by an emperor and a special class of landowning nobles. The government was centralized and asserted itself over a vast country, or empire. Other relics show that great works of art, especially those made of bronze, were already being produced in China. The fact that there was important art as well as a written language and a centralized government tells us that the level of civilization then was already amazingly high. This is particularly striking when you consider that people in Europe at that time were still living in primitive tribal societies.

The Chou Dynasty (1122–255 B.C.), founded by a conquering ruler from the northwest, followed the Shang period. During most of the Chou period China was split into virtually independent, warring kingdoms. But this was not the low point in civilization that it might seem at first glance. The various rulers of the dynasty realized that China was not functioning as a nation. To their credit, they allowed many questions to be asked about the role of government and the individual's role in society. The answers to these questions served to strengthen China again in later periods. The debates that went on during the Chou Dynasty were to influence both the course of Chinese history and also China as it exists today.

(29)

THE CONFUCIAN SYSTEM

The most important development from the questioning that went on during the Chou period was the rise of what is known as Confucianism. Confucianism is an ethical system, dictating relationships between individuals, between members of families, and between rulers and their subjects.

The system was devised by a scholar-official named Confucius, who came from one of the small and more or less independent Chou Dynasty states. According to tradition this man, whose life is surrounded by legend, lived from 551 to 479 B.C. Little is known about his personal life, but his teachings are considered by many to provide the key to understanding China. For a time these teachings were condemned by the Communists, who emphasized their own ideas about loyalty to the state superseding all other loyalties. But by the late 1970s, ideas of Confucius were being officially promoted again, just as they had been for most of the past 2,500 years.

Confucius always stressed the supreme importance of the family; this is the part of his system that is least appealing to the Communists. But he also wandered about from state to state advising rulers on the arts of government. Confucianism is often mistaken in the West for a religion, partly because myths surrounding the man gave him divine attributes and because temples and shrines were built in his name. But actually Confucianism was a practical system for maintaining order and governing a gigantic land.

In the Confucian system there were five key relationships. These were between ruler and subject, neighbor and neighbor, father and son, husband and wife, and brother and brother. Confucius taught that if these relationships were maintained properly, the state would function well. He also taught that all people should be acutely aware of their behavior and consider how others will respond to it.

According to Confucianism a person's very identity in the world depended upon how he (Confucius was mainly concerned with male roles) stood in relationship to others. Some would say that this is actually not very different from the Communist call for cooperation among all people for the sake of attaining common goals.

Confucius said that correct behavior was related to both education and sincerity. Recently, education suffered seriously as a result of Communist attempts to avoid the creation of a new elite class in modern China. But until the coming of the Communists, all successful rulers in China since Confucius's time had paid great respect to

Above: an artist's conception of the Emperor Wu (left) of the Northern Chou Dynasty. Left: Confucius was a scholar whose teachings later became the basis for many of China's values and morals.

Left: a bronze incense burner from the Han
Dynasty, a period which saw the end of
feudalism in China. Right: a Taoist priest
of prerevolutionary twentieth-century China
sits warming his feet on a portable warmer.

education. And in the late 1970s, a major effort began again to improve the nation's educational system.

As for sincerity and proper behavior, the followers of Mao and his successors have placed as much emphasis on a person's inner feelings as on his or her outward acts. This is why when Communist officials fall from power in disgrace they are expected to publicly confess that they have been guided by wrong thoughts.

Perhaps most important—even for today's Communist rulers—was the Confucian belief that if a leader behaved properly, his followers would too. The fall of dynasties in China was always attributed by the Chinese to the improper behavior of their rulers. This possibly explains why Communist leaders who fall out of favor are so harshly condemned. The behavior of leaders remains an extremely important subject to the Chinese.

HIGH POINTS OF CULTURE

Confucianism became conclusively established as the philosophy of the state during the Han Dynasty, which lasted from 202 B.C. to A.D. 220. This was a period of effective centralized rule and is considered the time when the firm foundations of China as a nation were laid. It was also during this time that feudalism, a system in which peasant farmers are virtually slaves to landowners, ended in China. Feudalism lasted in Western Europe past the fifteenth century and in Russia until the early twentieth century.

At the end of the great Han Dynasty, the central state again became ineffective in China. Bands of nomads roamed ungoverned through the agricultural lands of the north. Without a strong government, people everywhere were at the mercy of bandits. All over the country the system of government envisioned by Confucius was collapsing. At the same time, strictly religious influences, as opposed to ethical and practical influences, were becoming stronger.

Taoism, which began in China more as a philosophy than a religion, gained adherents. And so did the new religion from India, Buddhism. Buddhism, like Taoism, also started as a philosophy.

Both Buddhism and Taoism had strong mystical overtones, directly at odds with the practical ethical system of Confucius, and both preached that salvation lay not in making a success of earthly life but in renouncing the world. Through the centuries that followed, many destitute Chinese would cling to these religions as consolation

(33)

for their lack of material success. Others would adopt them as an escape from the chaos that existed in the periods between great dynasties and during the years when great dynasties were on the decline.

Yet these mystical religions kept a certain hold on the people even in the best of times. What was probably most typical of the Chinese mind was to accept both Confucianism and one or more of the mystical religions, and to follow one path or another depending upon immediate circumstances, all the while keeping the different paths separated and compartmentalized. Observers say that to this day, many Chinese people believe in both Communism and in traditional Chinese ideas—even where the two philosophies clash.

Mystical religions really asserted themselves during the period of chaos following the decline of the Han Dynasty. The chaos ended with the unifying Sui Dynasty, a short-lived dynasty that would be replaced by another long and great one—the T'ang Dynasty (618–906).

During the T'ang period the principles of effective government from the Han era were reestablished. The most formal system yet of examinations for government positions was adopted. The legal system was codified. Artists and poets created great works, and music and scholarship thrived, while lusty T'ang warriors continually extended China's borders.

Later, during the Sung Dynasty (960–1279), there was an even greater flourishing of the arts. The poetry became more exquisite, landscape painting attained its most refined form, and priceless art objects, such as fine porcelain pieces, were produced. The Confucian political system, which had been so successfully applied in the T'ang period, continued to guide the government of a centralized China.

At various times in China's history, dynasties were established by raiders from outside its borders. There was the Yüan Dynasty (1271–1368), which began toward the end of the Sung, founded by Mongol conquerors from central Asia under the leadership of the legendary Kublai Khan. The last dynasty, the Ch'ing (1644–1911), was founded by marauders from Manchuria in the northeast. Still, Chinese ways endured.

Foreign conquerors, in fact, always became absorbed into the Chinese system. The Mongols were succeeded by the native Ming Dynasty (1368–1644), and under the Ming emperors (whose tombs

**This bronze incense burner depicts
Lao-tse, the philosopher who founded
the Taoist religion, riding a water buffalo.**

Below: a Buddha statue. Buddhism started as a religion in India, but gained adherents quickly as it spread to China. Facing page: an artist's painting of T'ai Tsung, the first emperor of the T'ang Dynasty. Art, poetry, music, and scholarship thrived during the T'ang Dynasty.

outside Peking are considered one of the great sights of China), scholarship and the arts again reached new heights. The Manchus who followed eventually became so Chinese that they now can no longer be considered a different people.

THE OUTSIDE WORLD INTRUDES

Meanwhile, the Western world was catching up with the East and in some ways, particularly in the realm of technology, surpassing it. Westerners were eventually to make demands upon the Chinese and back up the demands with superior armed might.

The Chinese may still have considered themselves a superior people and their nation the Middle Kingdom. Westerners may, in the Chinese view, have been just another group of "barbarians" (the word used commonly by the Chinese for all foreigners). But by the nineteenth century, the Ch'ing Dynasty was in the process of disintegration, and Western barbarians were quick to take advantage of the situation.

The system of examinations for government jobs, known as the Mandarin (meaning "high public official") system, had become corrupt. More and more Chinese were questioning the ability and legitimacy of their leaders. There were armed rebellions against the Manchus, who maintained many privileges denied to their Han subjects.

Even more alarming, China was losing in armed conflicts with the Western powers. The first of this series of wars came when there was resistance to Britain selling opium, grown in the British colony of India, to the Chinese. The opium was creating a major drug addiction problem, and its purchase with Chinese silver was bankrupting the country. The British not only won the right to bring in opium, but they also won territorial concessions. They set up the colony of Hong Kong at China's southern tip, and many Chinese cities were made "treaty ports" in which the laws of foreign nations, not the laws of China, prevailed. Other European powers followed the British, and territorial concessions were also eventually won by the United States, Russia, and Japan.

A period of chaos, much like that experienced during the final years of all the great dynasties, set in.

The pressures were so great that in 1911 the Ch'ing Dynasty collapsed and was replaced, for the first time, by a republic. Dissat-

Above: this rare Chinese bronze figure
is seated on a fine carved wood
stand made during the Ming Dynasty.
Right: the crafting of priceless art
objects, such as this flower vase,
flourished during the Sung Dynasty.

isfaction remained, however. Disease, famine, and armed conflict plagued the country. Local rulers, known as warlords, using private armies, became the real governors of much of China. There were continuing economic intrusions and armed invasions from abroad, and eventually a civil war engulfed the entire country.

The civil war, with few interruptions, lasted from 1926 to 1949. In the years following it the triumphant ruling Communists would say that an entirely new China had emerged from the struggle. Others would say that the Communist regime was just a new, and in certain ways traditional, dynasty.

Chinese men smoking opium. Widespread use of opium created a major drug addiction problem in China in the early 1900s.

(3)

THE REVOLUTION

By the beginning of the twentieth century, many thoughtful Chinese were wondering if their ancient Confucian system of life and government was suited to modern times. The nations of the West, and also Russia and Japan, had made parts of the country virtual colonies. In a series of armed conflicts, foreign powers had humiliated the Chinese. There were scores of treaty ports inside China in which people lived by the laws of foreign powers.

Moreover, foreign ideas about the very nature of life and government were being adopted by many influential Chinese. China was ready for the first time in its long history to abandon its ancient imperial form of government.

THE NATIONALISTS AND THE COMMUNISTS

The imperial government had started sending students abroad, and many were returning with questions about the old ways. One of these students, Sun Yat-sen, became head of the new Nationalist People's Party, also known as the Kuomintang, which was the movement that in 1911 overthrew the Ch'ing Dynasty and proclaimed the Republic of China.

But China's troubles were not over yet. Under Sun's rule until his death in 1925, and later under the rule of the Kuomintang's Generalissimo Chiang Kai-shek, the Nationalists were constantly in a state of war. They fought the armies of independent warlords, the invading Japanese, and the Communists. Meanwhile, the hu-

Sun Yat-sen became head of the Nationalist People's Party, which overthrew the Ch'ing Dynasty in 1911.

(42)

miliating special status given to foreigners in China remained in effect, causing great discontent, until the later stages of World War II, when the West relinquished its rights mainly as a show of support for an ally against the Japanese.

The Communists ruled some parts of China for a number of years before they established the People's Republic of China—the official name of China under the Communists—on October 1, 1949. Yet their advance in the 1930s and 1940s, along with the civil war it promoted, was grueling; it was a struggle that produced national heroes who, both living and dead, are very much at the forefront of political life in China today. The greatest of them all was Mao Tse-tung, the man whom many historians compare to the emperors and founders of China's greatest dynasties.

Mao was born in 1893 into a comparatively well-to-do landowning family in southern China's Hunan Province. He was an avid reader from childhood and a lifelong author and poet. He was attracted during early manhood by both revolutionary ideas from the West and the forces struggling for reform inside China. He concluded early that the China he saw disintegrating around him could be saved only by a radical change in political philosophies, and Communism, he decided, with its radical view of abolishing private ownership of property, was the philosophy to be embraced.

An event that was central to the Communist struggle in China was the Long March, during which Mao established himself as the ideological leader of the Chinese Communist revolution. In October of 1934, after a series of clashes with Nationalist troops resulting in heavy Communist losses, the Communists found themselves encircled in the southern Fukien Province. They were forced to break out, and thus began the Long March, covering some 6,000 miles (9,600 km) in about a year and winding up, after numerous battles with warlord armies and the Nationalists, in Yenan in the northwestern province of Shensi. Only 20,000 of the 100,000 who started the march reached Yenan. They established themselves in now-legendary cave dwellings, where Mao rebuilt the party machinery while

Mao Tse-tung is considered by some historians to be the most powerful national hero of all time.

Above: the mist, reminiscent of Chinese landscape paintings, enshrouds Yenan, considered
a sacred place in memory of the Chinese
Revolutionaries who valiantly lived in nearby
caves after the Long March. Facing page left:
in Yenan in 1939, Chairman Mao talking with
young fighters of the Communists' Eighth
Route Army. Right: Chairman Mao standing
in front of the Yenan cave dwellings, the base
for the Communists after their retreat in 1942.

Above: Chairman Mao in 1946 working inside a Yenan cave dwelling, headquarters for the Communists after the Long March. Right: Chairman Mao taking part in physical labor at the construction site of the Ming Tombs Reservoir near Peking in 1958.

the Communist forces, sometimes in formal alliance with their old Nationalist enemies, concentrated on fighting the invading Japanese.

After the Japanese surrender in 1945, the Communists began sweeping through China, taking on their old Nationalist enemies. By 1949 they were in effective control of the entire country. They had driven Chiang and his Nationalist government into apparently permanent exile on the island of Taiwan, where Chiang ruled until his death in the mid-1970s, still claiming to be the leader of all China. The old rulers and landowners who stayed on the mainland were jailed, killed, or stripped of their possessions and sent to the countryside as workers.

Until his death in 1976, less than a year and a half after Chiang's, Mao remained a cult figure in the China that the Communists governed. Virtually every national event, from the smallest alteration in some purely local policy to the most sweeping nationwide change, was carried out in his name.

This does not mean, however, that the 1949 Communist victory resulted in a fixed new society with political institutions that would never change. Quite the contrary. Mao's goal was to create equality. He believed he could best achieve his goal by keeping the country in a permanent state of revolution. This belief is why scholars who look upon Mao as having been in the tradition of the emperors have so often been surprised at the startling social upheavals instigated by some of China's highest ranking officials that under Communism have been continually taking place.

A "PERMANENT" REVOLUTION?

From the beginning Mao and other Chinese Communist leaders spoke of what they called the New Democratic Revolution. Their emphasis was on land reform. Russia had theoretically based its Communist revolution upon its urban workers and saw peasant farmers as initially standing in the way of revolutionary goals. The revolution in China, however, was based on the peasant class. And in the first years of Communist rule, again contradicting the Russian pattern, many non-Communists, such as Madame Sun Yat-sen, widow of the great Nationalist leader, were allowed to hold high positions.

But later, non-Communists lost all influence. Mao ruled by what he called the "mass line," meaning that a leader goes to the people, the masses, is educated by them, and then returns and explains what he has learned to the bureaucracy. The Maoist program of *hsai fang,* the return to the countryside in order to learn, was an example of the mass line. This policy of learning and relearning from the peasantry was meant to result in constant change and hence a more equitable society. Unless Mao's fears that the Chinese would slip back into their old ways are understood, the seemingly sudden shifts of policy in China are totally baffling to the outsider.

Policy changes in China have frequently seemed contradictory, as if designed to catch the people off guard and prevent them from becoming complacent or losing their revolutionary fervor. But in yet another twist, after Mao's death China became more conservative and less revolutionary, and its leaders showed greater respect for tradition. Radicals who had surrounded Mao—including his widow, Chiang Ch'ing—were officially vilified and condemned. And in 1980 many of the highest-ranking members of the government, especially those from the Long March days, were replaced by younger officials.

Some of the struggles that characterize today's China inevitably involve clashes between personalities. Since the start of the revolution, some top Communists have advocated taking pragmatic steps aimed at rapidly increasing China's economic wealth. Others, including Mao when he was alive, have said that preserving revolutionary fervor to help achieve equality is more important than immediate economic gain. But even Mao wanted China to become a major industrial power and on occasion took some drastic steps to bring this about.

At one point during the 1950s, for example, Mao proclaimed that henceforth his nation would "let a hundred flowers bloom," meaning that the government would sanction a free discussion of all political, social, and artistic ideas. But before long, those who criticized government policies or actions found themselves labeled as "counterrevolutionaries" and were either jailed or sent off to work on communes or in factories.

Then in 1958, Mao proclaimed the "Great Leap Forward," by which, relying on the will of the peasantry, the country was suddenly going to become a major economic and industrial power. This was not to be accomplished in the usual ways. Perhaps most typical of how the Great Leap was to operate was the way in which China, at this point, planned to become a major steel producer. Rather than organize the building of modern steel mills near industrial centers, the steel was to be produced, in effect, by hand, in backyard ovens on communes.

Right: Chairman Mao (left) and Prime Minister Chou En-lai (right) applauding at a People's Liberation Army sports meet in the early 1950s, shortly after the Communists took power. Below: Mao's widow (far right) and the "gang of four" stand trial for treason and other offenses in November of 1980.

Partly because this new policy to leap forward economically involved so many small and scattered programs, and partly as a result of a series of bad harvests, the Great Leap ended in failure. China temporarily returned to a much more conventional approach to the economy.

THE CULTURAL REVOLUTION

By 1966, it seemed, as it did again in the late 1970s, that those who believed the most important goal was rapid economic progress had gained the upper hand. At the political forefront was President Liu Shao-ch'i, a long-time associate of Mao's from early revolutionary days. But now Mao set in motion what became known as the Cultural Revolution, which inside China was officially considered as important as the 1949 overthrow of the Nationalists.

After 1949, Mao, as Chairman and leading theorist of the Communist party, had gradually retreated from practical affairs and let others run things. Eventually the government, led by Liu as President, began to offer rewards, including special bonuses to workers with high production levels. Mao himself saw this as a step back to the bad old days, and he spoke of the danger of a "capitalist restoration."

In the mid-1960s a new theatrical play came to Mao's attention. The play was set during the Ming Dynasty but was obviously an attack on Mao for the way he had dismissed a high public official. The fact that the play had been permitted to run at all was used as an excuse for an all-out attack on the forces of moderation in China. Soon Chairman Mao, with the cooperation of his People's Liberation

Above: half a million people turned out in Peking for a parade celebrating the installation of Hua Kuo-feng as Chairman of the Central Committee of the Communist party of China, the post formerly held by the late Mao Tse-tung. Below: Teng Hsiao-ping, whom many observers considered the most powerful man in China in the years following Mao's death, speaks at the United Nations General Assembly in New York in 1974.

**Deputy Prime Minister Teng
Hsiao-ping (second from right)
meets in Washington with
President Jimmy Carter.**

Army (PLA), was rallying young people to his cause. All officials, including President Liu, who stood in the way of Mao's continuing revolution, were purged. Young students who joined the campaign gathered all over the country by the tens of thousands. Known as the Red Guards, they went on a rampage, destroying temples, old houses, graves, books, art objects—any symbol of traditional China. In the place of these objects they put up images of Mao. Liu and many other officials were arrested.

By the end of the 1960s, the nation was in such chaos that Mao told the Red Guards to go home and called in the army to take charge and restore order. But vast changes had taken place. Some officials were finished, but others who had been purged would later emerge into public life again.

Besides Mao, the only Chinese leader of world standing to ride out all the turnings of the Cultural Revolution was his long-time Prime Minister, Chou En-lai. Chou, like so many other leading Chinese political figures, was a Long March veteran whose success was due, in part, to the fact that he always managed to promote Mao's views and at the same time satisfy those who were looking for practical and efficient leadership.

Chou lived until shortly before Mao's death in 1976. In the days following Mao's funeral it appeared at first that the radicals, the people who had ridden so high during the Cultural Revolution, were now going to take charge of the government. But soon it became apparent that the more practical-minded—including many of those who had suffered during the Cultural Revolution—would triumph.

By the late 1970s, Mao's successor, Hua Kuo-feng, and Teng Hsio-ping, the Deputy Premier removed from power during the purge but now back in power, seemed to be succeeding in bringing greater stability and order to China. But it is unlikely that the struggles between those who favor a government designed primarily to move the nation ahead economically and those who favor a government bent on establishing equality even at the cost of keeping the country in a state of flux, are over forever.

(4)
TRANSFORMING A HERITAGE

An American journalist riding a train from Nanking to Shanghai fell into conversation with a government official, who began talking about how China had changed since the Communists came to power. "In the past," the official said, "the usual form of greeting was to ask, 'Have you eaten?' Now there is plenty of food, so we don't say that. The usual way to say good-bye was, 'Give my regards to your father.' That was because the father was always dominant in every family. But now that's not true anymore. The authority of the father is questioned every day."

There are, certainly, families in China who still believe in traditional values. And although most people eat well and nobody starves, there are surely those who do not get all the food they want. Also, there is some truth to the idea that the Chinese do not see the current regime as a radical departure from their past. To them it is just another dynasty, worth supporting because it provides an effective centralized government that meets the people's immediate needs. Yet at the same time, few traditional societies have experienced as many rapid changes as China did during the generation following the defeat of the Nationalists.

Familiar patterns of Chinese family life have been especially affected by changes under the Communists. For the first time in the nation's long history, women have been granted equal rights with men. Arranged marriages, in the past the normal practice, no longer exist, at least in the cities and on communes. The courts no longer enforce the Confucian relationships between members of a family. And since its inception, the government has been working hard to change loyalties from the family to mass organizations.

THE COMMUNES AND INDUSTRY

Probably the greatest changes for the individual have come from the establishment of People's Communes. These are collective societies

Above: women stonemasons, who
took part in constructing a new
reservoir, gather in a mountainous
region of Honan Province. Below:
members of three generations
of a Chinese family live together
in a workers' hostel in Shanghai.

Top: a team of about sixty workers, the basic unit
of the People's Commune, work side by side in
order to clear new ground. In the midst of them is
their leader, who is not supposed to be set apart
from the other farmers. Bottom: members of a
"production brigade" gather up silk cocoons made
by carefully tended silkworms in Chekiang Province.

Top: land on a commune is terraced for greater output and conservation. Bottom: members of a commune in Shensi Province go into a desert and plant trees to control the shifting sands.

in which Chinese farmers, which means the vast majority of Chinese, live. When they were first established in the 1950s, the communes appeared to many in the outside world as an attempt to reduce the Chinese worker to an ant-like, inhuman machine. Actually, commune life in general has turned out to be quite different from what most people imagined.

A People's Commune is a large organization designed to provide administration and set policy for an average membership of around 5,000 or 6,000, though a few are smaller and some have as many as 30,000 or 40,000 members. In such gigantic rural organizations, it is difficult to define all of the relationships between the members. The same is true of the "production brigades," averaging about 1,000 members each, into which each commune is split.

At the beginning, there were indications that communes would separate families. There was talk in the government of forcing members to live, regimented, in dormitories. However, things did not go that way, and in fact many traditional aspects of Chinese life, including an expectation that respect will be shown to elders, have continued in the communes.

In recent years, more and more emphasis has been placed on what are called "production teams," each of which has only about 150 or 200 members. The members are rewarded on the basis of their individual contributions to production.

Interested outside visitors are frequently shown a commune located north of Peking. Because this commune is often on display, its conditions are probably somewhat better than average. But foreign journalists who have made careers as "China watchers" say it gives a reasonably accurate picture of the communal life that most Chinese now live.

This commune takes in thirty-five villages, all of which were in existence before the commune system went into effect. Members of the production teams into which the commune is divided live in family groups that average five to ten members each. These family

With yields rising, due to recently introduced agricultural methods, farmers in East China dry newly harvested grain in the sun.

groups own their own homes—two-story structures that are often old but were substantially built and are kept extremely clean, with the outsides always freshly whitewashed.

The life is hardly luxurious. A bed is likely to be a brick oven with a straw mattress on top of it. Water is fetched from a nearby well. A single light bulb provides illumination.

Although most of their work is for the commune, the families are permitted to keep small gardens and a few animals, to provide extra food for themselves or to sell to the state for extra income. With the exception of these small family undertakings, the government buys the commune's produce from the work teams rather than from individuals; this encourages a communal approach to the people's work lives.

Recently the people on the communes have been allowed greater use of their private plots of land. And they have been given a greater say in what will be planted on their communes.

There is also greater flexibility now on how factories may operate. Instead of always being directed from above, factory workers can now make many more decisions on their own. Productivity rather than conformity to party line is stressed today. Increasingly, salaries of factory workers and also factory managers are being linked to a given factory's productivity. Bonuses are now frequently given as production incentives.

What is perhaps more significant is that China is now looking for outside help in modernizing its industry. This is directly against the practice, in Mao's day, of trying to be completely self-sufficient.

In recent years bankers from all over the world have been journeying to China to discuss financing of Chinese industrial development. There has been talk of setting up new factories as joint

Top: the General Petro-Chemical Works lights up the night at the Shengli oil field, one of the oil fields that is making China an increasingly important producer of petroleum and petroleum products. Center: this commune land is terraced for protection against floods and droughts. Bottom: women at work in a Shanghai factory that produces mechanical toys. This factory employs only women—700 in all.

Right: a new rail-
road cuts through
the mountains in
southwest China.
Below: tourist
groups from all
over the world
are now able to
visit China. Visit-
ing members of
an American
basketball team
stand on the Great
Wall. Bottom: a
modern hotel
(right) rises above
a public park
in Kwangchow.

Left: children take part in a spring outing by a lake in a park in Hangchow. Below: young children are given physical checkups at regular intervals at a nursery.

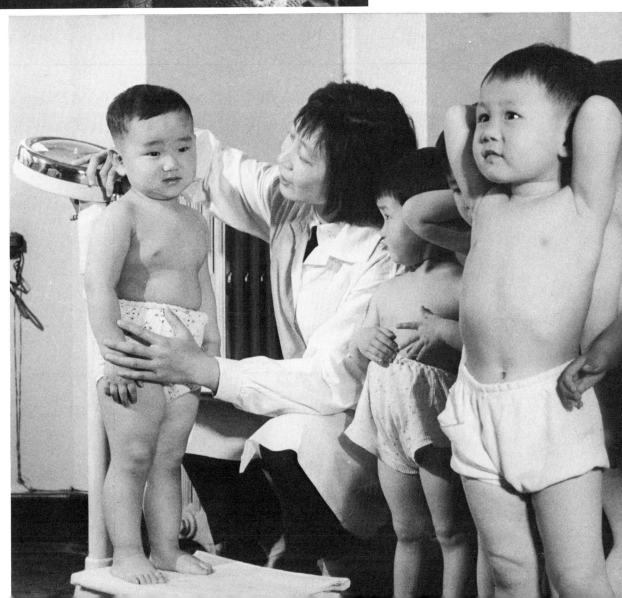

ventures with the more industrialized powers—nations of the West and Japan. Plans have been made to build new steel mills and railroads, and even some nuclear power plants, in cooperation with foreign firms. American oil companies are planning to assist the Chinese in their exploitation of offshore oil reserves. Moreover, there is more two-way trade than ever before; it is now commonplace to see Chinese goods in stores in the West.

And there is a new tourist industry in China. It used to be extremely difficult for most foreigners to get permission to enter China, but now tourist groups from all over the world are visiting. New hotels are being built. A Western hotel chain may soon move into China.

However, China is still Communistic, and there is still very little free enterprise in the country. For most Chinese, the communal approach to working and living predominates.

THE NEW EDUCATION

A key factor in propagating the communal approach is the education system. A Chinese child's first teacher today is more likely to be the state than the family.

On the communes, as in the cities, nursery school education is provided to children from the ages of three to five whose parents both work. Sometimes the children live at school, seeing their mothers and fathers only on weekends. By the age of five, the children are singing patriotic songs and repeating, with apparent enthusiasm, political slogans involving current ideas being promoted by the Communist party. If a faction of the party is in disfavor, the children

Top: kindergarten children in Inner Mongolia learn wrestling. Center: children gather for a rally in front of the Great Hall of the People in Peking's huge T'ien An Men Square. Bottom: by the end of their first year of elementary school, these children are expected to know 850 Chinese characters.

Left: these third-graders must dress warmly in class. They are learning how to read and write. Below: a dance is performed with care and precision by children at a kindergarten in Peking. Bottom: youthful gymnasts perform for their classmates at a school in Kwangchow city.

Right: in accordance with the government's emphasis on physical fitness, Chinese students now play basketball. Below: girls and boys practice gymnastics, a popular sport, at a primary school.

will shout against it, just as they will shout slogans against nations their government considers enemy states.

Sometimes in recent years, the favorite target of Communist wrath, as taught to children, has been the United States. But as relations have improved with the United States, the wrath has more often been directed at the USSR. Not only does China have border disputes with the Soviet Union, but the two countries are also divided by their frequently opposing views of what Communism should be.

More practical information is taught beginning at the age of six in the elementary schools. Language is heavily stressed. By the end of their first year of elementary school, children are expected to know 850 Chinese characters, and by the end of their primary schooling they must know 3,000.

In high school, mathematics and science are stressed, though a certain amount of time is still set aside for political indoctrination. Most classrooms have political slogans tacked on the walls. Books are constantly being revised to keep them in line with shifts in the official party position.

But most schools appear well equipped with workshops and laboratories. The students, sitting in pairs at wooden desks, are always attentive and polite. A typical school day is broken down into seven 45-minute periods, beginning with the reading and recitation of political works, going on to Chinese language and literature, then mathematics, agricultural biology, and other practical sciences, then music, both new and traditional. The last period is for marching and sports; particularly popular are basketball and gymnastics.

But the educational system under Communism is not so conventional as it appears at first glance, even taking into account the stress on political indoctrination. Committees consisting of peasants and workers, members of the Communist party, and students, control

Above: a student is not free to go on to higher education without the approval of the local committee. College students studying in the early morning at Tsinghua University. Below: soldiers from the People's Liberation Army help a rural People's Commune repair farm machinery.

primary and secondary schools in China. No matter how well a student might do academically, he or she usually cannot go on to higher education without the approval of the local committee. In the late 1970s, however, there were indications that this was changing and that the practice of preventing the children of the old Nationalists, merchants, and landowners from receiving higher education was ending.

Each year students undergo periods of military training with the People's Liberation Army. They also receive on-the-job training, sometimes in factories though more often on communes. This is a good example of the role of the PLA in modern China and also of the importance attached to learning from the peasants.

THE ARMY'S POSITION

One of the reasons that the Communist forces were successful in their rise to power was that Mao urged his followers, including armed and uniformed soldiers, to be "as fish in the sea." He meant that they were to join with the peasants rather than bully them, as had been the case before the Communists came, when no one was so despised as a soldier. One of the reasons the people turned to the Communists so quickly in the days after World War II was that the Communist soldiers, although outnumbered three to one by the Nationalist army, followed Mao's dictates so strictly.

Standing regulations for the PLA contain three main rules and eight "points." The rules are: (1) Obey orders in all actions. (2) Take not a single needle or piece of thread from the peasants. (3) Turn in everything captured. The points are: (1) Speak politely. (2) Pay fairly for what you buy. (3) Return everything you borrow. (4) Pay for everything you damage. (5) Don't hit or swear at people. (6) Don't damage crops. (7) Don't take liberties with women. (8) Don't ill-treat captives. Because the soldiers followed these dictates, a close bond was forged between the peasantry and the army. Communist soldiers have in general continued to be respected rather

Members of a local militia patrol with PLA in the wild country of Sinkiang.

than hated and feared. In 1965, just before the upheavals of the Cultural Revolution, all signs of rank, even insignia differentiating officers from non-officers, were abolished. Members of the PLA supported Mao during all the turnings of the Cultural Revolution and continue to play an important part in every aspect of life in China today, often working in factories and on communes in what would usually be considered civilian jobs.

Yet it is not the soldiers so much as the peasants who are officially exalted above everyone else in Chinese society. Students, even after graduation, and also their teachers, often to their disgruntlement, are expected to return to the land periodically to learn peasant virtues—just as high government officials are often sent to live on communes for purposes of "re-education."

The idea of learning from simple peasants rather than from an educated elite flies directly in the face of Chinese tradition—and is a strong argument that, whatever else is happening there, China is not just repeating its past.

THE ROLE OF CULTURE

The Communists, in recent years, have been somewhat more liberal about the past. In general, however, they continue to attack China's traditional culture. There have been times during the Communist period when China's ancient artistic traditions have been looked upon with pride. And many traditional arts are encouraged today. But there have also been occasional massive attacks by the state on what are looked upon as decadent cultural remnants of the decadent pre-Communist days. Although recently the old arts have come back into favor, at other times traditional drama, opera, and dance were replaced with dramatic revolutionary opera-ballets intended to teach political lessons.

Above: a weaver works in China's 2,000-year-old carpet industry. Below: a soldier from the PLA helps farmers repair a tractor in the shared rice fields of a commune.

(74)

After many years of absence, Chinese
opera has returned to Peking's theater.

**Apprentices learn handicraft skills in
Peking from a man who works with jade.**

These new works were seen constantly in live performances and over the nationwide television network. The best known, typical of many others, is the ballet drama called *Red Detachment of Women,* which was put on when former President Richard M. Nixon first visited China in 1972. The work uses modern music played mostly on Western instruments. While employing techniques of traditional Chinese drama, it is danced using classical Western ballet movements. It concerns a young servant girl who joins the Communists during the civil war after she is beaten up by a Chiang Kai-shek lieutenant known as the Tyrant of the South. At the end the girl leads an attack in which the Tyrant and his troops are wiped out.

The suppression of traditional drama, dance, and opera in favor of such propaganda works was to a large extent the work of Chiang Ch'ing, Mao's now-discredited widow. More recently such works have been played down, and respect for traditional culture, never totally lost, has been on the rise since Mao's death.

Although it is still difficult to find Chinese classics in bookstores, it is claimed that anyone who wants to can always study these works in community libraries. More and more, traditional arts and crafts, such as fine jade and lacquer work, are being produced without any reference to political themes. There are now many nonpolitical dance and acrobatic performances. And recently people have been encouraged to see and appreciate the great art works from the past, such as the old refined landscape paintings and bronze pieces.

Still, no great new works of art have emerged from China since the Communist victory. It is more in creating a better life for the people than in fostering high culture that the regime makes its claims for success.

THE STANDARD OF LIFE

One important aspect of any country's standard of living concerns the way its people eat. Although China has been slow to adopt chemical fertilizers and the more advanced forms of mechanization in modern agriculture, the country has been described as "a riot of food." Although in past years much of China suffered from periodic famines, new ways under Communism to distribute food, bumper harvests for a number of years, and the cultivation of ever more land

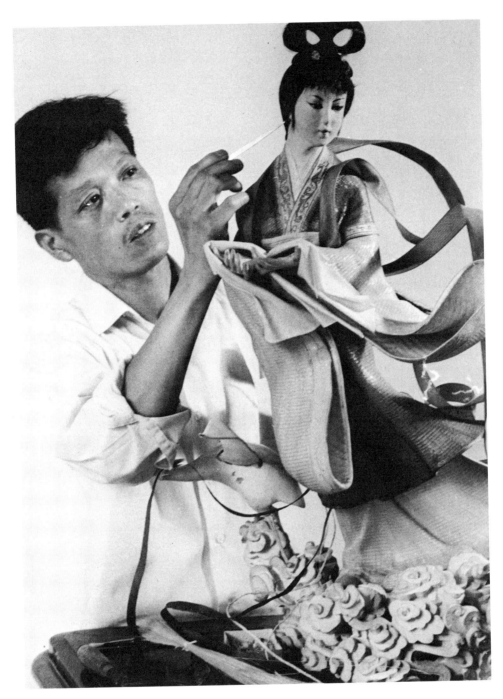

**An artist in East China puts the finishing touches
on a bamboo figure of an ancient goddess.**

mean that hunger is a rarity in China today. Moreover, most Chinese seem from time to time to be able to indulge in luxury foods for special occasions. And it might be noted that many Westerners consider Chinese cuisine to be the most refined in the world, topping even the cuisine of the French, which has long been considered the most refined in the West.

Consumer goods become more readily available each year in China, especially in the cities. Clothing still often appears relatively drab. This is partly symbolic, since people are expected to show their respect for hard work and equality. But it is also partly because cotton is rationed and the synthetic fiber industry is still in its early stages. Nevertheless, nearly everyone in China is warmly dressed in winter, even if the clothes are sometimes old and worn, and recent visitors to China's major cities report seeing more color than they expected, especially in women's clothing.

During the Cultural Revolution, fashionable clothing was banned. For years under Communism women wore gray or blue trousers. Their hair was either cut short or worn in pigtails. But now skirts and dresses are appearing again. Some women have taken to curling their hair and wearing bright blouses or kerchiefs.

For the first time in years, social events such as dances are being held. And it is now possible in China to see foreign movies.

Actual wages may seem low, but many people in China now have something to spare for luxuries. It must be remembered that in modern China food and clothing are extremely inexpensive, as is housing.

Moreover, virtually everyone now has access to free medical care. Medicine has made great strides in China in recent years. Hospitals and rural clinics are well equipped to offer the kind of routine medical care that was developed in the West. In addition, modern scientific principles have been applied to ancient Chinese medicine. Sometimes the hospitals and clinics use herbal concoctions and also

Members of an agricultural experiment group of Yunnan Province prepare an insecticide in a field. This group has been studying the outbreak of crop pests and successfully adopting various preventive measures.

Facing page above: cookies, cakes, and candies
are packed by workers at a bakery in Peking. Below:
hunger is a rarity in China today. Here, corn is
stacked for storage at a commune. Top: despite the
uniform drabness of Mao-styled garments, visitors to
China are beginning to see more and more color,
especially in women's clothing. Here, shoppers buy
brilliantly designed cloth. Bottom: a staff doctor
teaches paramedics the traditional healing art of
acupuncture at the Leyuan Commune in central China.

the ancient practice of acupuncture, which involves restoring the body's health and balance by pricking it with needles. Acupuncture is also used for anesthesia.

This emphasis on good medical care is in glaring contrast to the situation during the last days of the Nationalist government, when Chinese by the millions were dying from epidemics and plagues, long since brought under control by the Communists. It should not be forgotten either that in the old days famine was an accepted part of life in China and city streets were littered with men and women lying about, suffering from fevers, ridden with flies, or emaciated from smoking opium. These conditions no longer exist.

As for consumer items other than clothing, most people own bicycles to get about in the cities or on the communes, and many wear watches. Sewing machines—locally made, like the bicycles and watches—are common in Chinese homes. In nearly every group seen on outings in parks and at public monuments there is at least one Chinese-made camera. Although high officials have certain privileges, such as the use of cars, there are few other outward signs to distinguish rich from poor.

On the whole, the standard of living in China is lower than that of Eastern Europe, and even China's gigantic impoverished neighbor India has more cars on its streets. But this does not mean that, for practical purposes, the average person is poorer in China. In fact, because malnutrition has been overcome, and because the state gives each person security, the average Chinese is probably better off than citizens in most other developing nations.

Foreigners who travel widely in China talk of how much more easygoing life is for the Chinese than for people of other Communist countries. They talk of how a far greater spirit of equality prevails than in the rest of the Communist world, not to mention many non-Communist societies. It is frequently said that any regime—including

Above: doctors at a hospital outside Shanghai perform an operation while using the ancient practice of acupuncture instead of anesthesia. Below: cyclists and a trolley bus move along a street in the southern port city of Kwangchow.

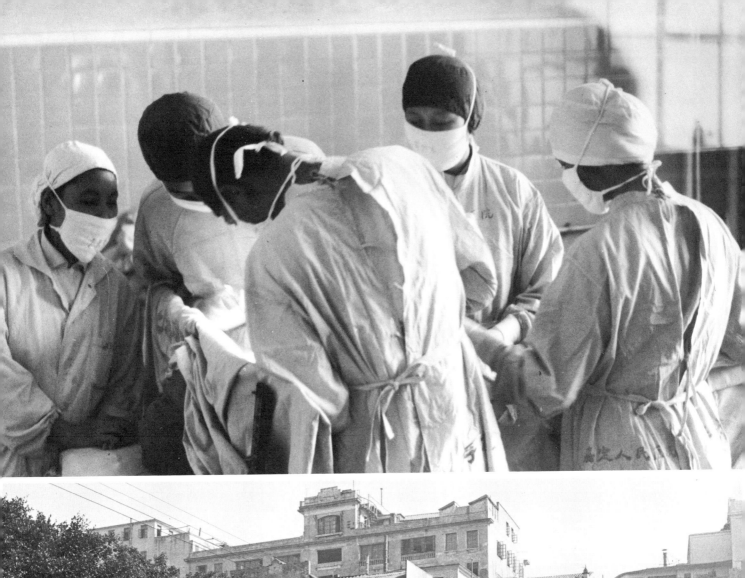

Facing page above: most Chinese people own
bicycles to enable them to get to and from work. In
this Shanghai street, bicycle traffic is a bit heavy.
Below: cameras are popular among the Chinese
people. This young boy is being photographed
in Peking's gigantic T'ien An Men Square. Top:
the Chinese delegation listens attentively at the
United Nations General Assembly in 1977.

the Nationalists had they had the luxury of a quarter-century of relative peace—would have accomplished great things in modern China. But that China under the Communists is experiencing a comeback in greatness and is providing for its citizens a better life than ever before cannot really be doubted.

While concentrating on building a new and better society at home, China has become increasingly accepted as a major world power. Most nations now recognize the Communist government, rather than the old Nationalist government on Taiwan, as the legitimate government of the Chinese people. Since entering the United Nations in 1971, China has been an active member of numerous international agencies. And before then the nation was engaged in intense diplomatic activity. Part of this activity was, and is, involved with challenging the Soviet Union's leadership in other Communist countries and in Third World, or developing, nations. But the challenge has generally been a peaceful one. The Chinese Communist line that has prevailed is that revolution must come from within. This means that the Chinese, for the most part, have not tried to export their revolution.

From all appearances, China has regained the self-confidence it had before the colonial powers intruded and again sees itself with pride as the world's oldest continuing civilization, possibly superior, but certainly unique.

INDEX